From a Mother to a Warrior

A Memoir

Terri L. White, LPC
Co-authors
GWhite, JWhite, GWhite, FWhite

KylaNicole Publishing

Powder Springs, GA

Copyright © 2019 by **Terri L. White**

All rights reserved. No part of this publication may be reproduced, distributed or transmitted in any form or by any means, without prior written permission.

Terri L.White/KylaNicole Publishing
Powder Springs, GA
www.KylaNicole.Org
https://www.terriwhite.net
Book Layout © 2017 BookDesignTemplates.com

From a Mother to a Warrior/ Terri L. White -- 1st ed.
ISBN 978-0-578444604-

Contents

Introduction 9
The Promised Land 10
Marriage Madness 20
The Roller Coaster Begins 31
Morphing Time 36
Time to Celebrate 49
God Is My Rock 55
Picking Up the Pieces 64
Sweet 16 76
A New Day 81
Warriors 104

 Introduction

This is a story about my journey as a mother of three children, a wife, a business woman, a student, and a Christian. Through this journey, I earned one more title that encompasses them all: Warrior. Throughout this testimonial it is my hope that you'll understand not only my journey, but also that you, too, can overcome anything no matter what's thrown at you!

Count it all joy, my brothers, when you meet trials of various kinds for you know that the testing of your faith produces steadfastness. And let steadfastness have its full effect on you that you may be perfect and complete, lacking in nothing.
James 1:2-3

All names have been changed for protection and privacy.

CHAPTER 1

The Promised Land

In 2008, I wrote and published my first book. I never thought it would bring such controversy, but sexual abuse in the church was a very difficult topic to disclose to family and friends. Since that book, my life has been on a rollercoaster; I will need to write a couple of more books just to tell it all. This book focuses on the challenges of having a marriage and raising children while serving God and trying to obey this awesome call on my life. But just when I thought we had survived it all, a major hurricane in our lives that encouraged us to move from Indiana showed me it was not close to being over.

After moving to Georgia, my husband George and I left our church after my first book was published and distributed. It was a difficult yet easy decision. The easy part was the level of frustration that led us to leave. I was hearing the same negative messages and experiencing the same strongholds that I felt in church before. Despite what I had been through spiritually, I was happy being under someone's leadership, but I shared with George that I believed staying in that church would make my book a lie because we had already broken free of negative leadership. We both believed that God had called us to ministry, but I struggled with the thought of pastoring a church.

I started school to get my master's degree in counseling for one primary reason: I did not want to serve people in the Kingdom of God without knowledge ("…my people perish for the lack of knowledge." Hosea 4:6). George and I had enjoyed working with couples and facilitating activities. I wasn't sure what direction God was taking me, but I knew it was going to be listening to and hearing from people. Once my book was out, people wanted to tell me their stories and I enjoyed listening and wanted to empower them with spiritual substance in order to break free of emotional scars and strongholds. George and I began working on our ministry. We believed there were too many churches "preaching" but not restoring people. We saw how people were being broken in the church. As people shared their story with me, I learned that deacons, ministers, and other clergy were spiritually killing families and, week after week, members would not be healed. George and I knew our ministry would focus on restoration. We began having Bible study in our home on Sunday mornings. Our goal was to not be an ordinary church with Sunday worship, weekly service, annual appreciations, and so on. We saw the need for marriages to be restored. We witnessed homelessness in the community. Children were struggling with relationships within the home and families needed to be taught how to love. So, Restoring Souls Ministry was birthed. Our first mission was preparing meals on the 4th Sunday of the month for the local children's shelter.

After about three months, we had already outgrown having worship in our home and needed a larger space. God soon blessed us with a small building to conduct our ministry. George's next vision was a food pantry. He was able to connect with grocery stores and other ministries to get food to give out on Saturdays. It was about 7 of us that would come and work the food pantry. It started with only a few people each week and we would have a lot of food left over, so we partnered with other ministries, giving them some of the food for their specific missions. One day, I sent a flyer to our local Division of Family & Children Services. That very next Saturday there were over 100 people lined up around our building and, needless to say, we were very overwhelmed!

We were passing out food but realized we were not feeding the people spiritually, so we developed a system for our small space. We would take about 25 people into the sanctuary and seat them, then I would call them back one family at a time to collect information. While they were waiting in the sanctuary, others came in to minister through song, prayer, and encouraging words. Meanwhile, volunteers in the pantry prepared the bags so that by the time I completed their information, the families were able to get their food and leave.

One challenge we had was the lack of knowledge about starting a ministry. As much as we wanted a seasoned pastor and wife to mentor and coach us, we were not able to find that. We were also not prepared to handle the financial hardship we were going to face. In our area, ministries seemed to be very territorial. I couldn't understand it because I felt that there were enough issues in the world that every ministry could do their part. With a handful of members, we were able to maintain from March 2007 to August 2010 in that location.

I got a job working as a Center Director for a Head Start and Pre-K program. It was exciting and exactly the type of work I always wanted to do. It built my self-esteem and confidence after what I had been through before moving to Georgia. My full-time job required me to work 50+ hours a week. I was in an online graduate program and I was setting up and establishing our ministry. We had three children and, at that time, Jessie and Jeremy were in elementary and our daughter, Hope, was in Pre-K.

Right after we bought our home here in Georgia, we were informed that General Motors was closing. General Motors is the company George worked for and how we were able to move to Georgia. We had to decide to either accept a buy-out to stay in Georgia or transfer to move with the company. We decided to take the buy-out. George was able to get a job at the local newspaper doing what he loved, printing the newspaper. Unfortunately, this job did not pay as much. After about a year-and-a-half, he injured his back which meant he was off from work. My situation never changed. I was still working full-time, going to school, active with 3 children, and building our ministry.

Life is full of unexpected events. George had to take a settlement for his back because he could not return to full duty. I knew his job would let him go, and being the planner that I am, I encouraged George to go to school or get a new certification in a trade that was not as physical while he was on workman's comp. During that transition finances were getting extremely tight.

In October of 2008, once he got the settlement, my only request was that we take a small portion to pay for a gospel celebrity cruise. We paid for it in full; got our airline tickets and I, being the very conservative person that I am, had put away a large portion of the money for spending and savings.

Within a few days after this, we, like so many other thousands of homeowners, got a letter from our mortgage company telling us our interest rate was increasing. George was working with the mortgage company to help us because our income had dropped and we were not able to make full payments. George soon got another job and this time the pay was significantly less than the last one. In the meantime, we kept getting letters of eviction. By February 2009, George was able to get a company to help us with keeping our mortgage. He paid the money to the company but we continued to get eviction letters. They told us, "That's normal. We are taking care of everything." This didn't settle with me, so I got the mortgage company on the phone with George and started asking questions. All I remember hearing was, "Your house had already been sold at auction. The sheriff will be at your house any day to lock it up." You cannot imagine the sick feeling that hit me. We had a two-story, five-bedroom house in an affluent community and, for those that know Georgia, they will sit all your belongings on the street. The eviction process in Georgia is very fast.

No emotional preparation, no moving preparation, no nothing. All I could think about was the kids coming home from school to a lock on the door. We had never been through anything like this, but I can say that it was very embarrassing, to say the least. I immediately went into "crisis" mode. I left work and stopped on my way home to grab as many boxes as I could. George and I both came home and literally started throwing things in boxes, emptying out cabinets and, of course, blaming each other. This is where our relationship took a turn for the worse. All we could tell the kids was that we were moving. For anyone that knows me personally, they know that I am a very strategic person — I like to plan and have a timeline and as a budget. But in this situation, we didn't even know where to begin. Do we just drive until we find a house? Do we look for an apartment? Can we even get an apartment with an eviction?

And yes, while all this was happening, I still had papers to write and books to read for school. Let's also remember that in less than three weeks, we would be leaving on a cruise. I remember walking through the drug store one day talking to my assistant on the phone telling her, how we are almost homeless yet leaving on a cruise in a couple of weeks — it didn't make sense. I didn't know how to tell my mom; I don't even think I told her the whole story. But we had to tell a few people because we needed help to move. I remember going to apartments and looking around and walking away crying. We had come so far. For the first time in our lives, we were able to buy a home for over $175,000. It had just been built; a dream house for us and, in a blink of an eye, it's gone. And yes, the $600 George paid the company to help us keep our home was a fraud! There is no other bad feeling in this world than being scammed.

In less than 5 days, we were driving around in a nearby neighborhood and saw a house for rent. We called and were able to get the house for less than what we were paying for our mortgage. Little did I know that the money I had saved from George's settlement would be needed for our move-in and we still had money left for our trip. In addition to that, the kids would be able to stay in their same school. At that time, I learned that there were thousands of people all over who were losing their homes, being evicted, and worse. While working the food pantry, I was able to meet people who had jobs paying over $50,000 a year and suddenly lost their jobs and their homes. With all that we were dealing with, we continued ministering to others, and I was still in school and emotionally exhausted.

The ministry became more difficult to maintain; we didn't have the money to keep it going. I had just completed our 501(c)3 nonprofit application but was not able to utilize it because we were waiting for approval. I started stressing about school and work. We eventually had to close the doors of our building, but we continued to distribute food and conduct couple's workshops.

Early in our marriage when we lived in Indiana, George and I attended a marriage retreat. That retreat changed our marriage, but it also started guiding our purpose. We had no idea that the awesome couple in Kokomo, Indiana, would have such an impact on our lives years later. During our time developing our ministry, we took advantage of classes that trained people to be Relationship Educators. We attended a 2-day Basic Training for Couples to be certified Marriage Facilitators. It was great! It gave us the opportunity to learn more about our own relationship and how to help other couples. Again, this was still driving my purpose.

My classes were getting more intense, I was on overload at work, and I was getting more stressed. George and I were having more tension in our marriage. Jessie was in high school and in the band, Jeremy was on the basketball team in middle school; and Hope was in elementary school in chorus and scouts. Our sons had been diagnosed with Attention Deficit Hyperactivity Disorder (ADHD) since elementary school. If anyone has a child or been around children with this disorder, you understand the frustration and challenge for both the children and the parents. What this meant for me is that I had to more closely monitor homework and classes, for not just one child but two. Education was very important for us. Our sons had never missed a day of school until they got to high school.

Two of the most challenging issues during this time was not having family around us and the embarrassment of feeling like failures. Although we seemed to be pulled in various directions, our faith never wavered. We stood on God's promise and his word, "I have been young and am now old, yet have I not seen the righteous forsaken, nor his seed begging bread." Psalms 37:25

It's important to know what God's word says and keep your faith strong so that you have something to stand on in times of hurricanes. That is what it means to be unshakable.

FROM A MOTHER TO A WARRIOR

Chapter 2

Marriage Madness

Before we moved to Georgia in 2003, George and I had a plan. We saw Georgia the same as many other African Americans: "The Promised Land for Blacks." During that time, many black people from up north were able to see other black folks as very successful people in Atlanta. Our plan was that once George got settled into his job and we got a home, he would go to school to become a home inspector as a back-up in case his GM job went away. I, on the other hand, had no intentions of going to school at all. Things didn't go as planned. I tried hard to encourage George while he was on workman's comp — that didn't happen. We talked about him going to school when I started school — that didn't happen. So, six years later, he was working a job that was hardly paying anything and he had no skill trade other than newspaper printing. This was a lot of pressure on me because from 2008 to 2010 the household was dependent on my income.

    I would like to take the time to be transparent. I have to admit that during this time I was a control freak. I would keep two and three bank accounts for emergencies. I never told George how much money I had but I always made sure bills were paid, the house was taken care of, and everyone had what they needed. When we first got married, we were not on the same page about money and finances, which caused a struggle in our marriage. There were many arguments about money. I came from a background where I always had everything I needed. I didn't know what it was like for lights or water to be turned off, or to be without transportation. I found myself feeling like I was always rescuing us in situations that he should have taken care of. It was aggravating. I felt that George was losing interest in providing for the family. He appeared distant, not motivated, and emotionally disconnected from me. In 2010, the arguments became more intense and I felt the marriage was not going to last. I began to hate him. The arguments would last for days of no talking, no touching, and complete avoidance. I can remember being in Virginia for school and talking to my friend telling her that I was wrong about the calling I thought God had on us because my marriage was failing. I couldn't see how I could counsel anyone.

We had been to marriage counselors, but I was not far enough in school to know how the process was supposed to look so I didn't know what to expect. Those counselors sucked! We tried talking to pastors that were older and nothing changed. At this point, I felt like we missed the ministry calling for working with couples.

One day after work, I met up with a co-worker for dinner. Like most women, we can talk for hours. When I came home that night, George had the nerve to accuse me of being with another man. I could not believe he would do that to me! Because I would not tell him where I was, he packed his bags and left, and then told our kids I had been with another man. This was unbelievable, I could not believe the direction our marriage was going. This even further solidified for me that I was in the wrong field.

After two days, he came home and we continued to have challenges. We were not talking but yelling at each other. Let me rephrase that and be real — I was cursing him straight out. Yes, we go to church and act like everything is all good, while we are so torn inside.

During this time, my course in school was Marriage and Family. I thought, "Good! I can finally find out what to do to change this man and make him straighten up." I cried through every single book I read. I was even angrier. Why? Because there was absolutely nothing in those books that informed me of what he needed to do. Everything was about me, my attitude, my behavior, and my way of thinking. I could not understand how changing my thinking and behavior would improve my marriage when he was the one with the problem. Further, I could not understand how I would ever use this in counseling. I started seeing signs of depression in George but, of course, he would never admit it. I was trying to apply the knowledge I was learning through my reading. It was working, but I was still struggling. The more studying I did, I was able to learn that, like my sons, I have ADHD and George has ADD. (For the experienced counselors that may be reading this, I know I am not supposed to self-diagnose.) It really made sense to me; everything in our lives started becoming clear. This new knowledge, however, didn't change our conflicted marriage. George still wouldn't talk to me. I thought I was his best friend, his right hand. I thought we were one, but he would not let me in.

During this time, Relationships Under Fire, a curriculum for married couples, was created. This curriculum was created from all the experiences we had in our marriage and other couples. When I had to do a project in school for an evidenced-based workshop for couples, it was right on time. I struggled with delivering this because of what I was going though in my marriage. I didn't feel that I was qualified to help anyone in their marriage. When I told my friend about the curriculum and the struggle in our relationship, she explained to me that

I am the test market for my product — you mean I actually have to go through this in order to know that it works?

By spring 2010, I tried having the conversation about me quitting my job. Work had become so stressful that I was crying every day on my way to and from work. I felt like I was being set-up on my job with my supervisor. Where I was once getting support, now everything I did was questioned. I had done so well with developing and cultivating the staff, meeting my obligations, reducing turnover, and boosting morale. But what about me? Who was there to support me?

George kept telling me to wait until he found something better, but I noticed that he was not looking, which was intensifying my level of stress. My mother was not coming to visit as much because she was caring for my grandmother. This made me feel bad because I felt I couldn't be there for her. My father's mother had also been ill, and he was not able to come support us either. He was stressed. Around May of 2010, I decided to make a plan for leaving my job. Again, the stress was the financial weight of the family was all on me. I knew that we would have to move again because we would no longer be able to afford to live in our rented house. I began weighing out my options of where we would live. George felt like moving in apartments would be going backwards but if he felt this way then I wanted him to do something about it. I felt alone in trying to decide what to do. I felt alone with trying to get through school because he would accuse me of putting school in front of him or the kids. He reminded me that I was creating more debt, but he never said anything about how the student loan refunds had helped pay bills or gave us money to buy the kids things they needed.

Meanwhile, I had learned how to complete an application for a nonprofit. We didn't have the money to pay anyone, so I spent hours researching grant writing, viewing webinars, and contacting companies to get funding for our ministry. There were two other women who also had nonprofits and we worked together trying to figure things out. No one would give us information. No one had the knowledge we needed. Eventually, I was able to get grants and funding to continue our ministry.

I felt my job was setting me up to fire me, so in July I gave my two-week notice. It was right then that I got a call from my dad and, for some reason, I knew what he was going to say on the other end. My grandmother had passed. At that moment I was not sad but angry — angry that my life was going in this direction and not feeling any support or love from anyone. My mom would be turning 60 in September and I really wanted to do something special for her. People who know my mother, knows that she does not like attention or anyone to do things for her. But this was important to me. It was important for me to try to give her something after all she does for my family. Keep in mind I had just quit my job, which meant the family was literally living on my savings and retirement money. Believe me, I know what all you financial people are thinking. A few months later for her birthday, I arranged for my mom to fly to Georgia to spend the week with us so I could pamper her. After picking her up from the airport on the way home, my car stopped. As if things couldn't get any worse, I needed a new transmission. I managed to have a good week for my mom but being the life saver that she is, she rented a car for the week while mine was in the shop. At this point, I am sure someone reading this is doing the math. That's right. No money to pay for the transmission or the car note. Oh yeah, no money to pay the rent either. By this time, George and I were hardly talking at all because there was no money and the handwriting was on the wall: we were getting ready to lose this house, too.

I was broke and broken. I was in awe that George never asked me how I kept the bills paid after I left my job; he didn't ask where the money came from for food. He would not suggest or recommend anything. He wouldn't talk about our situation; he only blamed me for quitting my job and not waiting until he found something else.

I have to give God credit for working out my car being fixed. When the auto shop called to tell me the bill was $1200, I told them, "I don't have it so you can keep it." No sooner than I hung up the phone talking to them, the auto loan place called to demand payment or the car would be repossessed. I told them, "I don't have it, come get it." Well, I then get a call from auto loan place again, this time they tell me they got a call from the auto shop and that they will pay the auto shop the $1200 and add that amount to my loan. They told me to come pick it up.

October 2010, we were moving. We were not just moving, but we were moving to a very, very small apartment. We had to sell most of our furniture because we wouldn't have the room. Our bedrooms had always been big enough for chairs, bed, stands, and more. This bedroom only had space for our bed. No back door, no balcony, no yard space.

We were barely in the apartment for two weeks when I got a call on my birthday that my other grandmother had passed. She had always been "super Christian" to me; never had anything negative to say about anyone. I had a hard time watching her struggle with Alzheimer's, and then she and my other grandmother both suffered from strokes. It was hard to watch my mother take care of her mother. My kids also saw a change in my mother but they were too young to know why. I was hurting for my parents while, all along, hurting myself.

Rock bottom for me was when a friend said to me one day, "Terri, you need to apply for food stamps and Medicaid." I was humiliated. And yes, I felt like I was far too good to be on welfare. I despised having to go to the welfare office with those case managers looking down on me like I was the stereotypical "welfare mother." I was the person always helping others. I was the person who tried to boost the self-esteem of others. I never in a million years thought I would see the day where I would be on public assistance. That was not the life I was supposed to live! I was so depressed, I cried for days at a time.

George and I were not on the same page and our marriage was still having issues. Living in such a small apartment, I knew the kids were figuring it out. We were trying to keep the ministry moving but it became harder and harder. People were still calling us for food from our pantry; they still needed housing assistance. I was getting more furious because here we are, can't pay our bills or keep a roof over our heads and these people are calling us for help.

George decided to try to go to school while he worked. I was very depressed. I hated we couldn't afford any extra-curricular activities for our children. They were hanging around the kids in the apartment complex, which was not good. The apartment complex was in walking distance to too many things that were not good. Our children were not used to living within the city limits. We wanted it that way for a reason. We were not going to church, we were not having church, and the boys were now both in high school. This was not a good combination. We found buildings, invested our money in trying to fix them up and ended up losing everything. I began losing interest in ministry. I was really beginning to doubt my faith, doubt God, and my purpose.

In July 2011, we were preparing to go to Indiana for the holidays. As I was watching TV one night, the Lord began to minister to me. I began praying and speaking in tongues as He spoke to my spirit. He began to show me that we were sitting in a roller coaster and He kept saying, "Buckle up...hold on...buckle up." I didn't know what to feel. It was a scary feeling of the unknown. I did not want to hear what God was saying. I wanted something else to come from my lips. Buckle up for what, what was about to happen? Why wouldn't God show me what he was going to take us through? Up to this point in our marriage, the challenges had been mostly about our finances, but I was not prepared for what was ahead of us. As God continued to speak to me, He began to show me how to humble myself to George. All of the studying I had done on marriages was now coming back to me. My friend said something to me that helped turn my whole marriage around. She told me to step back and allow George to have a relationship with God so that God could show him how to be a husband. She said that George didn't need to trust God because he knew I would always have a stash somewhere to bring us out. The hard part about this is that growing up, my mother would tell me, "Don't ever tell your husband everything you have. Always keep something put up for a rainy day." So, I felt I was supposed to keep that stash and, because his decisions affected me, I needed to make sure I had some comfort as well. For example, if the water bill did not get paid, that affected me as well, so I should have some money set aside. I was not used to being put in those positions. We went to Indiana in July and as soon as we came home from vacation, George got laid off.

In my work, I talk to a lot of couples, both young and old, who are ready to give up when their idea of marriage doesn't fit. Marriage is work and it can be very challenging. In many situations there is one person that is more concrete with finances than the other, but don't give up. When pressure hits your life, it forces you to evaluate just about every aspect of your life. For us, we had to make sure our marriage was right. As a wife, I began to learn some very valuable lessons. An important one being that just because you think it's right, it may not be the right thing for YOUR marriage.

It was only a few years later after our marriage was in a healthier place that George shared with me he was crushed and broken himself. He didn't know how to process what was happening with our ministry, our marriage, and our losses. In times like these when you realize how important it is to have people around you who can support you and speak life into you at any given time.

And let us not grow weary of doing good, for in due season, we will reap if we do not give up. Galatians 6:9

Terri L. White

Chapter 3

The Roller Coaster Begins

August 2011, I started my internship. I worked 10:00 am to 9:30 pm Monday through Friday and up to four hours on Saturday, without pay, while completing my last class of school. My emotional transformation begins. I had to shift my thinking, but I didn't know how. I had one mission: finish what I started — school. I was on the last stretch. The only income for the household is $250 per week. We sold plates out of our home to have money for personal hygiene items. George and

I started working on our marriage. It was challenging for me because I was controlling, I needed to know what was going on all the time, and I always needed to have things in place, but life was just not moving like that. We had to go to my parents for rent money practically every month. It was embarrassing. There were days I did not have gas money to get to work or get home from work. I only have one brother who has a mental illness and does not work a job. I could not ask him for money. No one in my husband's family would help us at all.

I can remember George asking neighbors for gas money just for me to get home from working my intern job. We had put all of our ministry furniture and equipment in storage and we lost it because we could not keep the payments. I was at the place where I was okay with all of it. I believed that when it was time for us to be functional God would open that door.

George followed through on every lead and applied for every job possible. He eventually stopped going to school. We were never able to reach Salvation Army on the phone for assistance or get any type of assistance for anything. We called family here in Georgia to see if we could move in with them while I completed school, which is not an easy request. But the alternative was our family of 5 living in a car. Every month, I called hotels to find out how many days we would be able to stay in case we didn't get our rent money. I felt we had tapped my parents completely out financially but no one else was helping us. They never complained or made us feel bad in any way. I had been applying for jobs with no idea how I would be able to work while completing my internship.

The kids were adjusting to a different lifestyle and did not know what we were really dealing with, but we tried to make things as normal as possible. George started talking to me and sharing with me more and more. I was co-facilitating a group with another counseling student and she showed the group a segment of the movie, "Secret." It was so interesting to me that I had to watch the whole movie. This added to my mind transformation. I shared it with George and we begin applying it. I made my first vision board. On that board, I took an old personal check and filled it in with the amount of money I wanted to make. I took old business envelopes and wrote my name on the front and wrote the word "checks" on it. I took a dollar bill and used a permanent black marker and wrote six zeros after the one. I cut out a picture of a home that I liked. I made graduation caps with my kid's names on it. I hung it up in my very small bedroom where I didn't have a choice but to see it every day.

George and I started trying to be proactive. We were looking for all kinds of solutions; we developed a plan. If neither of us could get a job before Thanksgiving, he and the kids would go back to Indiana, we would put our things in storage, and I would move in with a friend until I finished school and my internship in December. I need to say, moving back to Indiana was not something we wanted to do.

My sons began attending a church for at-risk youth. Our youngest son, Jeremy, enjoyed it and got involved in Christian rap and playing basketball. Meanwhile, our oldest son, Jesse, discovered love at 16. Our daughter, Hope, was maturing. I was concerned about her going to the middle school in our district. I wanted to expose her to an elite school. I found an all-girl's college prep school for her to attend. She was not too happy about it because it meant wearing a uniform and it was girls only. Hope was very respectful and a true "daddy's girl." I wanted a girl so bad and I enjoyed having a daughter. She spent every school break with my mother in Indiana. She and they boys would often ask to go live with my mother because they hated all the rules we had.

One day in November, I got a call for a job interview. I went on the interview a week before the holiday and was offered the job the day before Thanksgiving. The salary was $68,000 per year. Flexible hours, close to home, travel, insurance, cell phone allowance, all the works. Not only that, but it was learning how to obtain federal funding, contracting with the state, managing several contracts over a million dollars and hiring my own team all around Georgia. All of that was not even the blessing. The blessing was that they wanted me to start immediately after I completed school. I also got another job offer for community-based counseling, the very core of my studies. I had a decision to make and it would be a good decision either way. But when you've struggled the way we did, sometimes the decision-making ability gets cloudy. I felt that we needed the money with all the benefits more than I needed the counseling experience. So, the counseling career would be temporarily on hold.

The roller coaster ride was leveling out; we were emerging from the sharp turn. So, I thought this was finally over. At last, God was doing what He does best. George and I were doing better; our marriage was moving in a positive direction. We learned to take responsibility for our own actions and behaviors. We were able to pay our rent and bills. I took pleasure in cutting up my EBT card — never needing it again. I did well on my Comp exam and completed all my classes. December 2011 ended on an excellent note. It was amazing watching God manifest my faith in him once again. Isaiah 43:2, says that He will not let us drown or be consumed, and you, too, can stand on that.

FROM A MOTHER TO A WARRIOR

Chapter 4

Morphing Time

I started my new job, and George and I had a good rhythm. He managed the kids while I worked. I was preparing for my graduation. I had to take a final exam that was much like my Comp exam, but it was for the spiritual portion of the curriculum. I needed this exam to graduate, but I did not pass. I was thrown back when I didn't pass; it was unbelievable. I missed it by only four points. The hard part was that the school didn't tell you what you missed. The exam was all essay questions and based on a book. I studied and reviewed the material to retake the exam a second time — and failed it again by three points. I had one more shot to pass this test.

The letter I received from the school informed me that if I didn't pass the test, I would not receive a Master's in Counseling but a Master's in Human Services, which meant I could not become a licensed counselor. It was close to graduation, and I only had one more chance. I retook the test and was shocked to learn that I failed again, by only 1 point. I was just broken — I couldn't even read the rest of the email. Later that day, when I finally got the courage to finish reading it, I learned that I had 24 hours to complete a one-page essay on a question from the test which would be worth 10 points. Do I need to say more? It was not even a full day later that I received my congratulations letter of completion.

The boys were getting older and becoming more unruly. They were being exposed to the very activities that we had worked hard at keeping them from. The apartment complex had a lot of issues and people moved in and out all the time. This year, 2012, was going to be our year to recover what we had lost. I was able to start saving money for buying a house. We took a family vacation for the first time in about 5 years. In May, we traveled to my graduation in Virginia. It was great! I also did some traveling for my job. My daughter was preparing to start her new school at the Prep academy. Things were really looking up!

But nothing in this world could have prepared me for what was getting ready to happen. As Christians, when we say that we trust God, we need to make sure that we really do trust Him. Even though I had challenges to work through, I considered myself to be a strong Christian woman. But with every victory, the challenges would get stronger and it would appear that they were too big for God to deliver me. And like I said, nothing in this world could have prepared me for what was about to happen.

On a Monday in June, I came home from work early. I got a phone call from the assistant pastor of the church the kids attended. As the pastor was telling me what took place the day before, I completely lost my breath. Suddenly, it felt as though I couldn't hear. He told me that Jesse was caught with a girl and the incident had to be reported to the police. "Buckle up...the roller coaster is taking off again." We must have forgotten to get off the ride. When I told George, we both knew what this meant. I was enraged with Jesse — he had no idea what this one decision meant for his life or ours. Of course, my mind went to the worst-case scenario — but wait, the whole thing is the worst-case scenario. I was nauseous. I felt like a failure as a parent and a Christian. All I could think about was that God was punishing me through my son for all the things in life I did. Satan would show me how this was going to play out and it was not good.

Prior to this, I had done a study on morphing. We don't generally see it as morphing when we watch superheroes on TV but that's exactly what's happening. These are humans that live regular lives until something bad happens and they need super powers in order to fight the evil actions of others. These creatures are generally from another planet or another universe, which is what gives them their special powers. God began to let me know immediately that I am not from here. I have supernatural spiritual powers to fight what I don't see. The Lord began to show me that I could not get caught up in what was in front of me.

My mind went back to a year ago when God spoke to me about the rollercoaster ride and immediately, I remember Him saying, "Look at the cross and nowhere else. Do not take your eyes off the cross." My emotions were all over the place and I was struggling to pull myself together. We had never experienced anything like this before. I am a big advocate for child sexual abuse victims. I mean, did you read my last book of everything I had been through? I had to continue to go to work while trying to process what was getting ready to take place. I started searching for an attorney. I needed help. My son needed help.

This needs to be said: this is one area that many Black families mess up. I get it, most folks do not have the funds to hire attorneys. The cost is so high that retaining legal services is not the first option. But it is so needed. My God, I could not allow my son to fall into the hands of the justice system. I already understood the dangerous reality of mass incarceration. I knew how the system targets minorities. I knew that if my son were another race, the potential outcomes would look different. I could not be the parent that said, "He needs to learn his lesson and go through the process," or, "We'll pray and let God fix it."

Am I saying that what Jesse did was okay? Of course not. Am I saying that he should not be punished for his behaviors? Of course not. But I was not okay with him going to prison either. No, I was not going down either one of those roads. I am the parent that says, "We are going to save our son. He will not be another statistic; he will not be given to the system." He was only 16 years old and had no idea what all of this really meant. His whole life would be ruined like so many others. I have always had a soft heart for our brown boys, especially the ones that were in prison for one mistake or one wrong decision. It may sound like I am on a soap box, and I am, but the issue that I have with our criminal system is that they do not take into account that the brain is not fully developed until the age of 21. So why in God's name are we putting so many kids in prison, mixing them with adult murderers and molesters. I know there are some kids who are truly malicious murderers who have plotted and premeditated their acts, but not all.

So, we hired an attorney and the savings I had for our home...GONE! I cried... and cried... and cried... I worried every day. I was scared that Jesse would be swooped up by the police completely off guard and not having any idea of what to say or do. So, here we are trying to give a 16-year-old a lesson of his rights just in case he was arrested. And then, it got worse.

The company I was working for claimed to be a Christian company. In my position, I had to sign off on thousands and thousands of dollars, which caused a problem when I started identifying misappropriation of funds. I was the only black woman working that close to the CEO, and many of the managers I hired were black as well. Let me say, they were not hired because they were black; they were hired because they were highly qualified. But when I started confronting the CEO about the financial practices I discovered, I found myself being stripped of responsibilities and various accesses being terminated. I knew what this meant. Soon enough, I got a letter stating that my position was being eliminated. Interestingly, mine was the only one being eliminated. You know when the rollercoaster is making a drop from about three stories and a jerking sharp turn at the same time? That's what it felt like. We are now diving from $2800 bi-weekly to $300 per week. With legal fees added to the budget.

A few weeks after Jesse turned 17, we started getting calls from the police wanting to talk to him. Thank God our attorney had already educated us on what to do. One afternoon, when we got the call that we needed to turn him in. I thought I was prepared. We had prayed and prayed; I felt that God was going to have mercy. George went to pick him up from school. Again, we are trying to give him a crash course of what to expect. Who does this as a parent? Who starts teaching their kids what to do if you go to jail? What qualified us to give him a lesson? We had never been through this before; we didn't know people who had been through this before.

George and I took him to the sheriff's department and met the attorney, who informed us that Jesse should get bail and we would be able to get him out of jail within a day or two. We walked inside and the attorney took him away. We stood there, as to wait for him to turn around and come back with us. The officer told us to leave but I couldn't move. The only time we had ever left our kids was when they were with my mom. As we were turning around to leave, I could hear the officer reading him his rights and I turned back around. I saw him putting handcuffs on my son. It's been almost seven years and I still have the same terrible feeling I had then. George and I got in the car and, before he could drive off, a sound came out of me that I never heard before in my life. I was broken. My son… My baby. I tried to do the Wonder Woman spin, but nothing happened. I tried to turn into a Power Ranger, but that didn't work either. I tried to pray but nothing came out. What were we going to tell the other kids? Hope was still pretty young and didn't understand things like this.

That night, Jesse called asking when we were going to pick him up. Of course, all this happened on a Friday, so we would not be able to go to court until Monday. When we went to court, we expected to bail him out, and we could not have anticipated what would happen. I don't know how the families of high-profile murder victims are able to sit in court and listen to attorneys disparage their deceased loved ones. It was horrible hearing how they described my son. The judge never even looked up and as soon as the attorney got the last hateful word out of his mouth, the judge responded, "Bail denied." What was supposed to be a couple days turned into four months.

I finally begin to start morphing. I started learning how to use the power God had put in me before I was born. Once again, I started learning the meaning of trust. George and I were praying every day and speaking words to uplift each other. George didn't want any added negative energy coming into our situation, so we told as few people as possible. We only told my parents and my best friend. There was a part of us that was embarrassed. It was so difficult to talk about it. I had to learn how to be an attorney and a paralegal. I looked up terminology, I studied the court process, I researched all the information about Jesse's rights, and we talked to him every chance we had. I prayed for him every time we talked on the phone. It's sad that, as Christians, we try to teach our children Bible scriptures and how to pray for various situations, and they never use it until they get in trouble. But when you have nothing but time, there is more opportunity to read the Bible and understand it.

Money was getting tight again. The holiday was hard because our family was not together. Jeremy was becoming distant and combative. It wasn't until December when I got a job, thanks to a friend. My job was signing people up for the "Obama phones." George drove a van transporting my daughter and the girls to their school. We went to see Jesse every chance we could. I hated walking through that building. I could not touch him, we had no privacy, and we only had 10-15 minutes to spend with him. I would pray and cite scriptures every step I took to get to him. The attorney filed three motions to get bail and the same judge denied every single one, not even hearing the defense attorney.

I ended the year with a new job and starting my new career as a clinician for a private practice. In January 2013, we found a house for rent and I was able to save enough money for us to move. The roller coaster slowed down just enough for us to get off. We trusted that God was going to get Jesse out of this situation. My son had started going to the library and reading about his case. I couldn't get him to study and do homework at home, but I guess when you have time to make some life changes, reading law books becomes a priority. He informed me that his rights had been violated because something didn't happen within 90 days and would therefore have to be granted bail. This time, when we went to court there was a different judge. She made him wear an ankle bracelet, among other restrictions. Jesse was already struggling in school before this incident and now he would have to attend alternative school.

God has a reason for allowing things to happen when and the way they do. I learned some very powerful things throughout this process. I saw my son moving in the wrong direction. Jesse was not combative to us, but he was defiant and not following our rules. He had lost his interest in God, was failing in school, and started hanging around the wrong people. But while Jesse was incarcerated, I started seeing a man develop. I didn't like the way it was happening, but I did learn that God needs to do things His way and not ours. Many times, we want to dictate the way things happen for us, our children, and our loved ones. We have been taught by society that certain things are bad and there is no positive lesson to come out of it. Jesse had to learn how to pray and read the Bible when we were not around. He was finally able to understand the one thing we kept telling all of the children: there will be some situations mom and dad cannot get you out of. Jesse learned to speak his faith and declared what was going to happen. He had time to reflect and understand the consequences of decisions.

Life started moving to a new normal. Our new home was in a very nice neighborhood, and George was still driving the transportation van for Hope's school while he continued to look for a full-time job. At this point, he had not worked since his layoff in 2011 — the longest he had ever been unemployed. I took the state licensing exam for counselors and I failed. I did not feel bad because I had been out of school for two years. I just started a studying program to be ready to take it again. In the meantime, my work load was slowing down but the bills were coming consistently. By April, I was not making any money. So, here we are again.

This time I felt a little more prepared. I received unemployment again. I learned how to write notes for people who saw clients, which allowed me to make some money on the side. George started asking people in the neighborhood about cutting their grass. He would make just enough money to pay a utility bill. He continued to go around to the several elderly people in the neighborhood and they would refer him to other neighbors. His money slowly increased. My mom continued to help us financially. I knew that our van was soon to give out but I was still trusting that God would send us a vehicle. I didn't know how, but I believed he would do it. That summer, the van died. Thank God for my dad who brought us one of his vehicles and kept the insurance and registration up for us. All we had to do was take care of it.

Jesse was doing well in school, but Jeremy had become defiant and disrespectful. He had a girlfriend and was struggling academically. Not because he couldn't do the work, but because he didn't want to do the work. I tried to start him on the path for his future, but he was not focused. I started getting worried about him and hoped that he would not make any bad decisions. Hope hated going to the Prep school, but she was doing well. She had a very rigorous schedule where she had to be up with her dad around 6:00 am and didn't get home until after 6:00 pm most evenings.

In October, I rescheduled the counselor exam but I didn't tell anyone, not even my husband or mom, because I didn't want the stress of everyone asking me about it before I went to take it. I passed the exam and within a week I started getting job offers to work as a Community Based Counselor. I did not turn down one job; I worked three places at one time. I was determined that I was not going to be broke again.

God is surely a deliverer. We got a call from our attorney and learned that Jesse was offered a plea: probation, one year of jail time, and to temporarily register as a sex offender. He would also have to remain in school and complete his high school education. If he was to complete school before the end of his sentence, the judge would drop the jail time. I asked a lot of questions about the register requirements and restrictions. Living at home with his brother and sister would be the only exception, but Jesse would have to quit his job because of the location.

This is the very type of situation that I MUST give people hope for. I know how this was supposed to end; the way the system is set up to destroy another brown boy. It was nothing that we did to fix it; we didn't even have the knowledge of what to do. It was all God. Another lesson I learned from this experience is learning to hear people's stories. So many times, we are quick to judge people because of the label they have to carry. Jesse, as well as George and I, absolutely hated that he had to register. In jail, people automatically assume that registered offenders are nasty, dirty old men messing around with babies and little children. I learned so much about girls who are just as terrible as the boys. Girls lie, just like this one did. Girls are deceptive, and they do not understand the lifetime effects their words have on others. Unfortunately, there is no punishment for them.

If a young man age 16 or 17 is dating a girl who is 14 and they have sex, the parents can file rape, sexual assault, or molestation charges. That boy's life is ruined! I am not in any way saying that kids shouldn't be punished but I do not understand how only young men are being judged and executed for an act in which, many times, the girls have just as much responsibility. Let's not even forget the kids who are actually dating that have an age gap and it never gets attention.

Now, Jesse began counseling months before his sentencing, and the counselor asked questions about what lead him to need counseling. As we told her the story, she stopped writing and stated a name, asking if that was the girl. When we told her yes, the counselor immediately informed us that there was a conflict of interest and she would not be able to work with Jesse. She said that the girl had had a lot of emotional issues and had done the same thing before — luring older boys, making them think she is older than her age. The counselor said she was going to contact the prosecuting attorney to let them know about the behavior of the accuser.

Finally, closure to his case and everything could go back to normal. These types of issues are growing in our community. We must be educated as parents and educate our children as well. We must let them know their decisions matter and they impact the whole family. Our lives were unpredictable at that time. It seemed like everything was going to crash, however, God did it for us and He'll do it for you. You have to push past what you see and feel and know that God is bigger than any problem.

Chapter 5

Time to Celebrate

I have not shared much about the middle child, Jeremy, so this chapter will mainly focus on him. I tell him all the time how he gave me the best pregnancy. Jesse came early, gave me preeclampsia, high blood pressure (that has never been controlled), and he had a heart defect which caused him to have surgery at nine months, and me with phenomena. Hope also came early and gave me congestive heart failure. But Jeremy was full-term. I was able to experience my water breaking, labor pains, and all the other wonderful things about pregnancy. He nursed without any problems at all.

FROM A MOTHER TO A WARRIOR

When I told my mom that I was pregnant, she was so upset because of the complications from the first pregnancy. I remember her telling me that she didn't think she could love another grandchild as much as she did the first one. I am here to say she is stir-crazy over each one in his/her own special way. My mom is the best friend to each of them.

This is the one child everyone had a nickname for. I started calling him Buster Boy because he was so juicy despite being a preemie. At the age of 22, we still call him by his nickname, Buster. Jeremy was so crazy about his dad as a baby, he cried every time his father was not around. As I was feeding him in his high chair one day, I noticed that every time I handed him food, he would switch hands and put it in his left hand to eat. I was so amazed because I wasn't familiar with left-handed children and didn't know it would be discovered so early.

At the age of 2, he was fascinated with listening to preaching. This was the one time in church he would sit still and be totally engaged. At home, we noticed that he would start replicating the pulpit. The funny thing about this is that Jeremy stuttered badly and could not pronounce a lot of words, but when he preached it was very clear. By the age of three, he wanted to wear suits every day. He would refuse to leave the house without a shirt, tie, and jacket. At church, he would go straight to the front row and sit until the end of service.

Jeremy and his brother were very close. They slept together, played together, and could not be without each other. After we moved to Georgia, he adjusted well in school. He was very social – sometimes too social – and a class clown. We discovered he had ADD in the 3rd grade but he adjusted well. Before he began his freshmen year of high school, Jeremy wanted to play football. We did not know how much time that was going to take away from his studies and he struggled once school started. By the end of his first semester, Jeremy had failed nearly all of his classes. Because he and Jesse were not putting a lot of effort into school, I threatened to take their regular clothes from them and make them wear a uniform. As they continued to struggle, I took all of their clothes and gave them each two pair of khaki pants and three polo shirts, and they had to wear plain black shoes. Things began to look up from there.

As a young child, Jeremy didn't talk back much. He was my sensitive and emotional child that needed minimal discipline. It wasn't until he entered the teen years that we started seeing more defiance from him. He and Jesse were starting to fight more, and that was one thing I did not tolerate.

One time when we were on a trip, Jeremy threw a tantrum because he wanted his cell phone. We were not — no, let me correct myself and keep it real — I am not that parent who just freely gives my children any and everything just because they ask for it, or because it's the most popular thing to do. During this time, teens were starting to carry cell phones and

George insisted on getting them phones against my will. So, we are in the car and Jeremy is in the back seat demanding to get his phone back. I was so outdone by his behavior that I told George to pull over the car. I snatched Jeremy out of the car and gave him a good going over. By this time, he was eye to eye with me. He did not seem to be submitting himself to me, so I slapped him dead in his face – don't judge. The look he gave me said, "now what?" My mind immediately went back to the National Black Parent Anthem: "I brought you in the world, I'll take you out!" I knew from that day, I was going to have to go in on him full force.

Another time he took me to a very unholy place. While living in the apartments, as I described earlier, I was not in a good place emotionally. I could hear cursing and yelling from another room that was unbelievable. I ran into the front room and this boy had the nerve to curse his brother like he was the "HNIC" (I am not going to tell you what that means). I started swinging and, before I knew it, I was cursing him out. And yes, we are a Christian home. George heard the commotion and jumped in. George has even less tolerance for back-talk than I do. For the first time, George hit one of our kids with his fist and Jeremy went down! Although George and I have had our disagreements, the one solid rock we stood on together was kids being respectful. I feel another person rising up inside me when my kids are disrespectful.

Needless to say, when Jeremy found a church with a big youth program, we supported him. He developed a love for singing and rapping. He was very social and filled his time with church activities. At 15, he had his first girlfriend and we knew when she broke his heart. I can home from work one day and Jeremy was sitting in the car alone, crying his eyes out. Shortly after the breakup he was okay. He then started dating a minister's daughter and I started seeing more positive changes. As we approached his senior year, I began to worry about him graduating on time. I was having school meetings all the time; I had to stay on top of him about school work and the disrespect came back with a vengeance. With everything we had going on with Jesse, we now had to watch Jeremy and his behavior. He would not follow the curfew rules, he wouldn't clean up behind himself or do chores; he didn't care about his hygiene and he had an explosive temper. By the time graduation came around, George and I were ready for Jeremy to start his next chapter.

It is a wonderful feeling to have a child graduate from high school, but I never thought it would be something that we would have to pray for. I thought it was something that was an expected, natural, normal thing to do. Jeremy did not have a plan and it appeared that nothing I tried to do was working for him. George and I sat Jeremy down one day in June and told him that he needed to make a decision about his next move by July 15. He had three choices: 1) Military 2) College 3) Full-time job. Even though I tried to help him with the process, we saw the handwriting on the wall when Jeremy was not taking care of his business to get into college. This left the military or a full-time job. With the process of elimination, we knew that he would most likely not get a job making enough money to live on his own, so he enlisted in the Army and scheduled to leave at the end of December 2014. Finally, we had one kid out of high school and heading to the military, one trying to complete high school while working a job, and a middle-schooler.

We tried to love on Jeremy as much as we could because we knew he would be transitioning into a very different life than what he was accustomed to. He started calming down just a little. During the Christmas holiday, the guys stayed home while Hope and I drove to Indiana. When we came back, it was time for Jeremy to go to basic training. We were celebrating with many good transitions. Life was good! God finally allowed us to get off the rollercoaster

Chapter 6

God Is My Rock

As we celebrated the coming of 2015 by sending Jeremy to basic training, we were also preparing for Jesse to complete his last year of high school. But Hope began to struggle. Because she appeared to be in so much distress about private school, we started her 8th grade year in August 2014 in public school. Before she left the private school, I was concerned because she was becoming very sassy. Hope excelled academically; she had friends and was very social, but emotionally she complained about being depressed all the time. I had taken her to counseling, but it wasn't working. She would always tell us she wanted to live in Indiana with my mother or that she wanted to go to a foster home with parents who would love her. I enjoyed doing mother-daughter activities with her like getting our hair done or going to the movies. Yes, I did work a lot, but I made sure to take time for the kids, George and the family.

Our home had a good balance. I worked mostly all day, so George would see the kids off to school and often cook in the evenings. At dinner one evening, there was a big disagreement between Hope and I about what we had cooked. I'd had enough of her telling us she was going to leave and never come back because of how badly we treated her. I told her to get her stuff and go. In our county, there is a program called A Safe Place, which is a designated business such as a gas station where kids could go if they were running away or if they were in trouble. A volunteer would pick them up and take them to a shelter with other kids. I took Hope to a local QT and told them to come and get her. Her mood and appearance were cold and shut-down. I was very angry at how she described our lack of love for her. My mom was also shocked and hurt. Hope had spent every single summer, spring break, and almost every Christmas break with my mother since we moved to Georgia. She and my mom are best friends but even my mother could not talk her out of it. This was the first time I had ever experienced Hope being so cold and distant. She had thrown tantrums before but not like this.

Hope was gone for a couple of days. When I picked her up, I didn't have much to say. I probably could have handled the situation much better, but all of my counseling training and education was not working in this situation. I did arrange for us to get in-home intensive family counseling; we all needed it. Things did not quite go back to normal. Hope started going to church with her brother but I had a lot of reservations about it because of what happened to Jesse at that church. I realize that it was not the church's fault, but you know how when you don't have a good experience at a restaurant you never want to go back? That's how I was feeling about my kids attending there.

So, here we are, February 2015. My mom is in town visiting. She is a great mediator and is able to keep things calm around the house. I really thought we were out of the park with the rollercoaster. But not a chance, it was time to buckle up again. And once again, I was not prepared. One evening after church, I was taking Hope to a youth activity. She wanted to go to the mall to see a boy that she met at church. Well, I'm not sure what parents allow a 13/14-year-old girl to go to the mall to hang out with boys, but it wasn't going to happen in my world. Hope became very angry when I told her that she was not allowed to go. My mom and I took her home with George and we left to go to the store. When I came back, George was asleep and Hope was gone with a note on the bathroom mirror. George and I drove all over looking for her. I called the minister at the church she visited to see if they knew anything about the boy Hope was talking about. They didn't know anything but offered to come to the house. When George found Hope and brought her back home she was insistent on leaving. She stood at the door with her suitcase. My mom was in disbelief at her behavior. When the minister and his wife came over, they offered to take Hope to their home for the night thinking that she just needed time away from us.

The next morning, when Hope came to get her stuff for school, I hugged her and tried to talk to her. George and I went to work and my mom stayed home with Jesse who was in a home-based school program. I got a call from Hope's school counselor asking me questions about issues at home. The counselor told me about resources for clothes because Hope had been getting clothes from the school and telling them we were not buying her the things she needed. I was so taken back.

That day, I came home from work early as I was expecting a mental health assessor for Hope. During this time, my job was very stressful. I provided in-home counseling and all of my clients were at least an hour commute. I was driving and praying, and God began to speak. He didn't warn me, but He did speak. When I got home, Jesse's teacher was still there and, shortly after, the assessor arrived. Hope comes in and I don't even know who she is. While I am trying to talk to the assessor, she is in her room screaming and crying "I hate it here!!" It gets worse. As I walk to her room, I see a man at the door and it is Child Protective Services! He introduces himself to me and tells me about a call regarding Hope and an accusation against her brother.

When I tell you knowledge is power, but God help us, we did not have the knowledge this time. As my whole family is being questioned by CPS with a mental health assessor and a school teacher present, Hope is laid out in her bedroom on the floor treating us like we were complete strangers, I was still holding onto the fact that God surely would not allow this weapon to form. Instead of knowing how to assist Jesse with exercising his rights by not allowing him to talk to CPS without an attorney, we knew beyond a shadow of a doubt that there would be absolutely nothing that they could charge him with. GOD IS MY ROCK, HE IS MY FORTRESS, IN HIM WILL I HIDE. I had to go to my room and hide in Him for just a minute. I walked in my bedroom and I said out loud, "Not this time Satan. Not this time. I will pass this test. I will praise you God no matter what."

When I came out of my room, the CPS worker said, "we have enough for just cause, I will need to call the police." Jesse had no idea what was even happening; he was completely clueless. The police arrived and asked George to take Jesse to the police station so they could talk to him. Again, knowledge is power. I don't care what anyone in this world tells you, DO NOT EVER TALK TO THE POLICE WITHOUT AN ATTORNEY! It is never "a little talk." Everyone went to the police station except me and my mother. I waited up for George, Jesse and Hope to get back home. When George walked in the house without Jesse, I just walked into my bedroom, got ready for bed and went to sleep. My mother was completely broken, not because she thought it was true, but because she couldn't understand why this storm had hit.

No, I was not in denial. Yes, I did believe something was going on with Hope, but I knew it was not that. The next morning my mother took Hope and went back to Indiana, she knew my heart could not take too much more. Jesse called and he was torn, broken, confused, crying, and he kept saying over and over, "why is my sister doing this to me? Mom, I told the truth, I would never ever do anything to my family. Has anyone ever heard of 'crimes of similarity?'"

In less than 24 hours, my house was wiped clean with no one but me and George left to figure things out. Less than two years ago, we spent over $5000 in legal fees and here we are again. Tax money that was earmarked for a down payment on a house once again is being spent on legal fees.

And yes, while all this is happening, I still have to get up, get dressed, go to work and listen to everyone else's problems. Clients that have been raped, depressed, have Schizophrenia, parental issues, school problems and all. Not to mention that in a few weeks, we would be going to see Jeremy for the first time in three months.

After she and my mom were gone for about three weeks, Hope insisted on coming home to talk to us. This was difficult because of so many emotions. My mom was overwhelmed with trying to deal with Hope while listening to me and feeling all of my emotions as well. My mom brought her back and they stayed at a hotel. Hope was trying to talk to me but I was in so much pain that I just didn't know how to be there for her. I had to ask her point blank if she really believed that her brother did something to her. When she said "no," I knew she had no idea what all this really meant.

At this time, we were allowing a Public Defense Attorney to take his case — DON'T EVER DO IT! We took Hope to see the attorney and they took her statement. When we went to court, the prosecutor said we coerced Hope and she would not make up something like that. George was working that day and the prosecutor asked, "Where is her father? Does she have a father?" This was simply horrible.

Family Day for the Army was scheduled in March, just a couple of weeks before Jeremy's graduation from basic training. This was supposed to be a family trip to celebrate with him. Instead it was me, George and Jeremy's girlfriend. It was so hard going to see one son locked up while trying to celebrate with another son for such awesome accomplishments. It was also difficult not being with my daughter while at the same time not wanting to be with my daughter.

When it was time for Jeremy's BT graduation, Hope and my parents came, and we went together. It was so exciting to see one of my children make such a major life transition. It was also so very difficult because my oldest son was not able to share the experience with us. Jeremy was talking about getting married. George and I were expecting to hear this conversation but not so soon, and not at graduation. I was a ball of mixed emotions. I wanted so very much for the tension and anger between me and Hope to end.

When the kids were younger, my mom would ask me if she could keep them. I remember thinking, "these are my kids; I would never give them away." I asked God for each one of them and I knew that God had equipped me and George for parenting them. But at this time of my life, I struggled to believe that I was destined to have kids at all. I felt like a complete failure.

We brought Jeremy home after graduation and he wanted to ride with his girlfriend. What was happening here? When we got home, we hardly spent any time with him over the weekend. Jeremy only had a week before he had to go to his duty station in Kentucky. We were excited about him starting his life independently. That Sunday, he informed us that his girlfriend had become his fiancé and they were planning to get married the very next day. This was a totally different kind of ride. This rollercoaster was not even in the right park! I'd already had so many major transitions with the family and now my baby, who is barely 19, is getting married.

We did not get invited to the wedding at the courthouse. George and I were sitting at home Monday afternoon and Jeremy and his new wife came in. I was not angry, I was heartbroken. I was so hurt that I couldn't embrace him. I went to my room and cried all day. My best friend had to help me pull it together before Jeremy came home from his honeymoon. Some situations really do feel like it is the end of the world and that life will never be the same. It's true that life may never be the same, but it is not the end of the world. God is a keeper and He will keep you and your mind if you allow him to. I realized that in order to keep my son and be in his life, I had no choice but to accept his wife. I have talked to many couples where a parent will not accept their child's spouse and this is not acceptable.

Chapter 7

Picking Up the Pieces

Hope stayed with us the summer after Jeremy's wedding but it was still very difficult. We continued to have challenges with her being disrespectful. Her behavior started a sequence of calling the police because she would attempt to run away from home. At the beginning of the school year, my mom came back to pick her up.

Jesse's attorney informed us that we were able to get a court date and asked Hope to come to court to speak on his behalf. At this time, she was beginning to see the impact of her decision, but I still don't think she fully understood. I knew this because she wanted to see her brother, she missed him and she wanted to go back in time and change what she did.

My mom brought Hope for court. It was a scary experience because I didn't know what to expect. The judge finally agreed to give Jesse bond but Hope would have to stay with my mother in Indiana. Jesse was released after being incarcerated for six months for something he did not do. Six months may not seem like a long time to some but for a young man trying to follow the rules, work a job, and finish high school, six months is a very long time. Not only that, his time for probation had to freeze. A few weeks after he was out, I got a call from the attorney that all the charges against Jesse had been dropped.

Jesse came home and tried to pick up the pieces of his life again. We were attending church at a local ministry. My job had been pretty stable, and I was able to go from working as a community counselor, driving all over the city, to working in the office. I learned something about myself: I loved my freedom. I took advantage of the time I had for a 9-5 job and started formulating my practice. I had also been working on my credit. For the first time in over five years, we actually had more than $100 in savings.

George and I started talking about buying a home. In October, I found a new community being developed. When we went to the open house, the finance officer had us feel out a credit application and we were approved to have a home built. That very day, at that moment, we picked out our lot. The saleswoman allowed me to make a payment plan for the earnest money and down payment.

I took the paper home and tried to calculate some numbers for when and how much. We had to have $10,000 down in order for them to start building, and the remainder had to be paid within three months of completion. I had no idea where to get that kind of money. I needed to raise my credit score another 40 points in order to qualify for down payment assistance. I went to work that Monday and started praying that God show me how to make this happen. No sooner than I completed the prayer, a coworker came to my door and asked if I knew anyone who wanted to make some extra money doing clinical work. You would not believe how God sent me through a whirlwind, working weekends, nights and early mornings.

Before I got my first check, I got a call from the saleswoman telling me she was sending pictures of where they started preparing the lot. God allowed me to make each payment on the date I set until just before we closed, and I owed $3,000. I never had to touch my regular pay check to make the deposit and our move-in date was March 3, 2016.

Before we moved into our home, Hope came back home right after Thanksgiving against our advice. We knew the court did not want her back home because the judge had released Jesse in our care and ordered Hope to stay with my mother. When she came home it was very awkward because Jesse was home. The first time they saw each other was at church. The pastor and his wife were instrumental in helping the family start the healing process. I must say that Jesse has a very forgiving and loving heart. George and I could see that he was very hurt but Jeremy was willing to forgive his sister.

An issue we had with Hope coming home early was that it did not give us a chance to get Jesse a place to live. This is significant because the first time Jesse was in trouble, when they gave him his sentence, I asked the attorney to clarify what this meant for our family since Jesse was still a minor and needed to live at home with my other two children. We were told that Jesse could be around no other minors other than his siblings. But because we did not get this in writing from the judge, it didn't exist. So, when the second accusation was made, and we went to court, the prosecuting attorney accused me of being a neglectful mother for allowing my child to live in the home with a registered offender. Please let me remind you, I already had a report against me from CPS about my daughter's allegations. And yes, while I am a Licensed Therapist. After that experience and because we did not have a judge's signature, we knew we needed to find another place for Jesse to live. I contacted his attorney and we went to court to at least get the judge to sign a paper stating that Jesse could be around Hope in the presence of parents.

Moving into a new home meant a new school for Hope. We were struggling with how to split the two children. After one month of her being in school, I came home early one day from work and got a phone call. Child Protective Services AGAIN! This was like a nightmare that would never end. This time, a report was made that I was allowing my daughter to reside with an offender. As if that was not enough, probation officers were threatening to lock him up. Of course, Jesse was terrified. I had to have Hope go stay with a friend who lived less than two miles away. Meanwhile, her attitude is still disrespectful and oppositional.

You may wonder why we didn't just have Jesse leave. He was over 18 at the time and limited as to where he could live. He barely made enough money to pay a phone bill, let alone pay rent. His name could not be on anything that would require a background check.

So, do we need to have a conversation about how the system is set up for offenders to violate probation or why there is a high number of people with a background being incarcerated. Again, the legal system is NOT designed for people to make it out. Parents, please talk to these brown boys and girls about how their conduct affects them and their families even when they try to do better.

Within a few days, we found Jesse an apartment not too far from us. In response to this allegation, Hope and the family had to have counseling. We were all interviewed and were told by CPS that, "children don't lie about things like this." Earlier, I talked about the rollercoaster ride we were on. This time, I felt like we were riding on the wing of an eagle. I had another lesson to go through; God was teaching me how to stand on Him and not be moved by what was to come.

That summer of 2016 went fairly well. Hope had started in-home counseling and went back to school in August. She met a friend at school and a friend in the neighborhood and they were talking about going to homecoming. Her behavior was pretty stable. She was very consistent with coming home, eating, talking to us and then going to her room to take a nap before doing homework. She continued to tell us that she was still depressed and had been ever since I had made her go the all-girls school. The psychiatrist decided to put her on an antidepressant and I noticed an immediate change. She started taking walks in the neighborhood that lasted 30-40 minutes and would not tell us where she had been. We would drive all over the neighborhood looking for her. I would get very scared because I didn't know the people in our new neighborhood. So, I couldn't imagine whose home she would be in.

One evening as I was coming back from a walk, she was coming from the opposite direction walking with a boy and it was pretty dark outside. I didn't say anything about it because I wanted to see if she would. I reminded her about the rules of not being out after dark. A few mornings later, Hope was getting ready to leave to catch the bus, but she was trying to leave the house early and it was still dark outside, so I told her to wait until her bus came. I went back upstairs and when I came back down, she was not in the house. When I opened the front door, she was talking to the same guy I had seen her with a few days ago. Have you ever had that feeling as a parent when you see someone for the first time, you know that person is up to no good? I told him she couldn't be outside until it was time for her bus and I made Hope come in the house. This turned into a huge altercation. I gave her several warnings to stop being disrespectful and that if she didn't do what I said she would not be going to homecoming the next weekend. I went in the house for a few minutes, when I came back, she was gone.

I didn't see her anywhere. I jumped in the car and drove to the bus stop, and there she was sitting on the curb with this guy. I told Hope to get in the car and when she refused I informed her she would not be going to homecoming. I could not believe her defiance. The next day was Saturday; I was leaving for work and noticed Hope was not in her room. This was strange to me because she has always been a late sleeper. While I was driving down a block away from my house, she was just casually walking around. I had to detach myself emotionally because I was preparing to see clients. It may sound cruel, but in my line of work, and being self-employed, I could not take days off. George had already left for work. When I got back home around 1:00 pm, Hope was not home and I could not find her anywhere in the neighborhood. It wasn't until 9:00 pm that I was able to find her. I just happened to hear some kids laughing as I was driving around and I spotted her and a few other children sitting at an empty lot. I told her to get in the car and she refused, so I called the police.

I couldn't believe I was in this position. This stuff doesn't happen to families like ours, or so I thought. When George got home, he was furious. The boy she had been with lied to George and said he had not seen my daughter, yet he had been with her. Hope's behavior that night was unimaginable. She started cursing and refused to come in the home. The police officers had to aggressively threaten her and told her they would arrest her if she left the house. This girl acted like she was on drugs — this was not my daughter.

By this time, I was numb to everything that had been happening. The therapist in me grabbed a calendar and started charting her behavior. We called her psychiatrist and had Hope taken off the medication immediately. A few days later, I got a call from the school telling me I had to come and get her because she was feeling suicidal. I felt more frustrated than concerned. I was frustrated that his rollercoaster ride would not end. I was angry that I didn't know why this was happening. I was broken because I felt I had done so much to try to show all my children love, support, and compassion.

I listened to Hope in counseling. I tried to give her what she stated she needed from me; I didn't know what else to do. She did not have a problem with my mother, her dad or brothers, just me. I had to take her to the psychiatric hospital which was even harder for me. When Hope was released, she still didn't want to come home or go back to school.

FROM A MOTHER TO A WARRIOR

When Halloween came, Hope asked her dad to go out with a couple of kids in the neighborhood. George and I don't believe in Halloween but we let her go. It was after 8:30 pm when we called the police because she was not answering her phone. Hope was nowhere to be found in the neighborhood. She walked in the door about the same time the police arrived. It was difficult for me to refrain from snatching her in front of the officer. She was smarting off again. After the officer left, we took Hope's phone, tablet and other electronics.

The next day was my birthday and I had worked all day. When I got home, Hope was demanding her phone and electronics. When we would not give them to her, she started knocking things over, yelling and screaming. This was not my daughter. However, I'd had enough. Jail or not, it was time for her to get SLAPPED. George tried to restrain her because she was getting out of control. We sent her to her room and not even an hour later the doorbell rang. Not just the police, but the same officers. They got a call from someone in my house saying they were being abused. I wasn't sure how that happened since we didn't have a house phone and her phone was taken. George and I told the officers we whipped Hope and we told them why — and we also told them that it was not against the law in Georgia. The officer asked to speak to Hope and looked her over. He told us, "Good job, keep doing what you're doing."

I already knew how this would play out the next day so early that morning, I called the school counselor and told her what had taken place and that I was fully aware Hope would report being abused. It wasn't even 8:30 that morning before I got a call from the counselor informing me that they had to contact CPS again.

At this point, George and I had agreed to let her go to the state. Hope hated living with us; she felt that we were abusing her and didn't love her. She claimed to be depressed living in the house with us and that we did not allow her to do anything. I had to go to the school to pick her up because, once again, she reported feeling suicidal. When I got to the school, I had no idea CPS would be there. I told the social worker that George and I were prepared for her to be removed from the home. I had my calendar of dates and events and I told her point blank, "I will not have a child living in my home being defiant, disrespectful, and telling me what to do. Yes, I slapped her, and we are ready for you to take her." To my surprise, the lady looked at me and said, "Mrs. White, we can't take her. She is in a loving home, she is not in any danger and she needs you and her father." Because she was suicidal again, I had to take her to the hospital. This time, I walked in, signed the forms, answered questions and left.

Okay, all my fellow clinicians, I can hear you now. Yes, I went to therapy. I tried looking for a mentor. I tried looking for programs and other support. I tried putting Hope in some kind of activity. She refused. But I can't stop now, it gets better and better. Sometimes it really does take detaching. George and I didn't so much as answer the phone or make one visit. The numbness was becoming more profound.

The year ended on a great note. I was able to move my practice into my own office suite. I helped Hope get caught up with some of her classes; she is so smart and does extremely well in school when she applies herself. She began complaining about the kids in school bullying and teasing her. We tried to talk through it. I was not sure how much was Hope causing drama and how much was actual bullying.

February 2017, these episodes went on and on. At one point, I had to start taking anxiety medication. My stomach was in a knot all the time. I could not believe this was my life. It seems like we had to call the police on a regular basis. Let's not forget, George and I had to continue working our jobs. I was back working as a community counselor, driving all around the city while also working at my private practice.

On April 10th, Hope went to school from my mom's house. Late that afternoon, my mom called and told me she didn't come home from the bus. There comes a time in a Christian's life that you just say, "Damn!" Jeremy called me late that night to tell me Hope is on a bus headed to him. She stayed with him for a little less than a month. From the time she left my mom in April to May, Hope had not been in school. She realized that she was not able to go to school where Jeremy lived because he did not have custody of her. Wow, so we were a little smarter than her after all.

During this time, finances were good, finally. My practice was growing. George and I were able to do a weekend getaway and it was much-needed. My mom came to visit and gets a call from Hope asking my mom to come get her so she can come back to Georgia and get in school. I figured something was wrong because she complained so much about not going to school here because of being bullied. My mom went to get her and turned around and came back in one day. School was almost out but I took her to register anyway. The very next day, I left her with my mom while I went to work. At 12:30 that Wednesday afternoon, my mom called and told me Hope went for a walk. We did not hear from her again until that Friday night when the police contacted us. An officer who caught her and a friend stealing at a grocery store ran a check and saw them in the system as runaways.

I was so relieved, I went home first to see George. I picked up Hope, so upset because they wouldn't arrest her, and I didn't open my mouth until the next day. This thing called parenting is real and sometimes you'll have to walk away and revamp with God. Don't ever think you have it all figured out. Each child comes with a different set of guidelines and you'll just have to follow God the best way you can. Once you've taught them everything you can - prayer and guidance is all you can give.

Chapter 8

Sweet 16

Hope's 16th birthday was quickly approaching. She made it very clear that she was going to drop out of school when she turned 16. She was already falling behind for missing so many days. We had discussed earlier in the year that she could have a sweet 16 party, however, those plans changed when her behavior escalated. I'm not sure why she was so surprised and upset. We still allowed her to get her hair and makeup done and take pictures for her birthday.

Hope insisted on telling us that she was going to drop out of school and that she was going to just stay home. I asked her where she wanted us to take her because we do not support high school dropouts in our house. We are not the kind of home where parents work hard, and adult kids lay around without a job, not contributing to house work, not in school and not handicapped. Hope took that to mean that we didn't want her.

Hope finally started doing better. She was going to try to go back to school. She was trying to talk things out more. Some friends of ours came to visit in June and we went to Hilton Head for the weekend. It was great getting away. Hope took summer school classes to try to catch up with classes. It was great feeling some sense of stability. The whole family took a trip back home in July. There were times when I felt that things were too good to be true, something must be getting ready to happen. It was time for school to start again. We had talks about making changes and focusing. This was supposed to be Hope's junior year but she was almost one semester behind. We got through the first few weeks of school and then Jesse was in a bad car accident.

The three of us went to the hospital. Jesse had to stay overnight. We were planning to take Hope to the county fair the next day. I went to work that morning, then to the hospital to pick up Jesse. When I got home, no one was here. I called George to see if Hope was with him and she was not. I knew this was not getting ready to happen again. Not again. Things had gotten so much better. We waited until midnight before calling the police and filing a report, hoping she would pop back in the house. We did not hear from her at all. Jeremy contacted me and informed me that Hope and her friend were there in Tennessee. At this point, I was so done with everything. Hope was gone for four days. During this time, I was getting calls from her friend's mother and family looking for them. Jeremy. told me he had talked with her and she agreed to come home and straighten up but when she came back to Georgia, she didn't come home. Her friend's mom was able to track them down and asked me if I wanted to go with her to pick them up. It was a "no" for me. I was ready to explode.

Oh yeah, did I mention I was full force in my private practice? No days off. George's business slows down in the fall, so I have to pick up the financial slack. We were preparing to take a cruise in October and I was planning a big 50th birthday party for November.

It was close to midnight when Hope got home. I was infuriated by the fact that she didn't want to come home. I felt like it was a big game to her and she did not realize the danger of all of this. Not to mention the situation she put her brother in and the length of time we had been going through these struggles. I remember going to her room and asking her a question and the demeanor in which she responded set me off. I tried to take the paint off the walls! Things went flying and breaking. When I heard her tell me she was going to call the police on me again, I escalated even higher. I called them myself and told them to come get her or take me.

We got through that night and a few more days of school until one day Hope did not come home right after. It took my best friend calling Hope's phone and laying into her. Hope and her friend finally arrive at home full of lies. Again, just a foul attitude and no apology. She was supposed to have tracking put on her phone a few months before but had not done it. She was on my parents' plan and they struggled with turning off her phone because it was our only method of contact when she ran away. In expressing my disappointment and frustration to her (and yes with the use of profanity) about the choices she was making, she continued to be defiant. George and I had been planning a night out and, even with all my anger, we stuck with it. I told Hope's friend she needed to leave, and George and I left. As if the matter couldn't get any worse while at dinner, it did. At this point, we locked the doors and went to bed and left her and her friend outside. We didn't budge. Yes, she slept outside some place all night.

So, for all you parents that are struggling with defiant children and are trying to reach out for help, here are the facts for Georgia:

There are no more "unruly child" charges. The minor has to commit an actual criminal act such a murder, assault, etc. Shoplifting or robbery has to be a minimum amount.

There is also no longer a juvenile detention center in Gwinnett County. The children go to jail for minors and there are very few locations spread out throughout the state.

There used to be a law against runaways but that has changed as well. Too many children in the state are running away and there is no place to take them. Parents just have to keep calling the police in hopes the child will turn up alive somewhere. If you have the time and connections, you can try to have a family judge listen to your case and possibly get your child in court. Keep in mind that Georgia has the highest number of teens involved in sex trafficking. I was told over and over that our issues were a family matter and the court would hold me responsible. But on the other hand, if you spank your child and CPS is called, you will have a case against you.

There are no "scared straight" programs. No camps for children with behavior issues. No mentoring programs. And remember, we are parents that care. What about the ones that don't have any resources, or single-parent homes. Hope finally called my mom again to ask if she could go back to stay with her. I was completely against it because of what she had done the first time. Hope was our responsibility and my mother should not have to deal with all the drama. My mom and George agreed for Hope to go. Against my wishes, they got her a ticket and sent her back to my mom.

If you're reading this and you do not have children or you have adult children, and you have a passion and heart for families and youth, you are so needed. I truly felt like I was at the end of the road and when Hope went to my mom, it gave me a reprieve. I was able to breathe again. I realize that everyone doesn't have a mother like mine. If you can be that person to help someone, please reach out. The blessing is that she got in school, worked a job and gave my mom no problems.

Chapter 9

A New Day

In writing this chapter, you have no idea how thankful I am at this moment that God brought us through all of that. George and I were able to go on our cruise a few weeks after Hope left and it was much-needed. Statistically, we were not supposed to make it. Both of us coming from divorced homes, neither of us experienced watching a healthy marriage. In September 2018, we celebrated 25 years. We have learned how to love, be in love, and make love. I celebrated my 50th birthday in November 2018, and I had an absolutely great time. In December, I then took another BIG step of faith and expanded my practice into my own building! I started my

Doctoral program at Capella in January 2019 and I am so excited to see how God will continue to use me.

Jesse was able to meet the one requirement for his probation that he struggled with for the last five years: graduate from high school. He had been in GED classes and had a very hard time. It was a client of mine, who I believe God sent my way, who told me how she went to Penn Foster to get her high school diploma. Why do I say God sent her my way? I had never thought about Penn Foster before speaking with her and I never saw her again. I called the school immediately and got Jesse enrolled. He was only six classes away from graduating and it took five years, but he completed his program in only two months. We could not go to his graduation due to the cost of taking a whole family to Pennsylvania, but we did have a graduation party to celebrate. Everyone that makes that milestone accomplishment should have a cap and gown and it was my honor to get that for Jesse. We are looking forward to nothing but great things in his life.

Hope is a different person. Immediately after she went back to stay with my mother, she got a job and started a program that helped her catch up her classes. We had no issues at all when she came home to visit during breaks.

In July 2018, Hope and I went on a weekend trip to Florida. The first time ever just her and I. She will be a senior in high school in less than a month and we are very proud of her. I don't know what the future holds for her, but I do know that God has her.

Jeremy is serving our country and nothing in this world makes me prouder than when I see him in his uniform. Yes, he makes decisions we don't like, but our love for him is so much stronger. Because of my son and his wife, I get to change my name in February 2019 from Mom to Nana.

God gave me faith. I'm tearing up now thinking of the many times I felt I couldn't hang on. So many nights I cried uncontrollable tears. There were days I just couldn't do the "Wonder Woman spin" and even when I tried, I didn't feel like a superhero.

I cannot close this book without giving a special "thank you" to my wonderful, supportive mother. She has been the rock for my family. George sees her as just Mom, not a mother-in-law. Our kids call her and love on her and talk to her about anything. I don't think I could have done any of this without her love. My father has also been awesome; in the last five years, he has come through for us every single time we needed him.

The next four mini-chapters are from my husband and each of our children. I asked them to contribute to this book so that we can help families by letting them know that every family, every parent, and everybody is going through something. Some issues are more challenging than others, but they hurt all the same. Be encouraged! Stay in faith and continue to walk in your truth. You must practice self-care, surround yourself with support and most of all have a relationship with God. He was and is my refuge, shelter, and bridge over troubled water. If it was not for the Lord, I don't know what I would have done. After you have done everything you know to do, just stand!

From Hope...

My parents wished for me, dreamed about me and prayed for me to be born. After several years they finally got their little girl. They told me that before I was born, they had bought everything pink for the nursery. They informed me that my whole birth was fully thought out. As I look at the pictures from the day I was born, I saw that so many people were at the hospital, but I really don't remember many of them because we moved to Georgia just before I turned two.

My favorite memory as a child was my 8th birthday, it was a slumber party. I had friends and they always made me feel accepted and wanted. During that age, things were good with my family. We had a dog that I absolutely loved. We also lived next door to a family that had a daughter my age and we were really close.

When I was a teen, my mom and I were not close, especially when she forced me to go to the all-girls school. I hated her for that and we became distant. I hated going to a school with all girls, uniforms, hormones and just not getting along. The teachers were horrible there. I was able to start going to public school in the 8th grade.

My father is the greatest. He and I were extra close and I loved going to the daddy-daughter dances with him. We would have date nights and I always felt like he loved me and that I am his priority. He was not a deadbeat dad. He does whatever he needs to do to make me feel happy.

FROM A MOTHER TO A WARRIOR

My oldest brother is Jesse. We were not really close because there is a seven-year gap in our ages. My brother Jeremy and I bonded a lot but there was a gap in our age as well. Jeremy would watch TV with me and it seemed that he related to me much more than Jesse. Jeremy used to fight for me when my parents did not allow me to do things.

The most hurtful time in my life was when I made a false accusation about my brother. When I came home from school, there were social workers, counselors and police officers. It seemed like everyone had lost their minds. When all of this happened, I left to go live with my grandmother. I finished my 8th grade year and started my freshman year away from my family. I didn't realize how bad that would make me feel. I remember always wanting to go live with my grandmother, but it didn't feel like I thought it would.

Another hurtful time was when Jeremy came to visit during a Thanksgiving break. He came to the house to visit me and asked if I wanted to go to the store. I met up with a boy at the store that I liked from school and we were very inappropriate with each other. When I walked out of the restroom, I was looking dead in my brother's face and I'll never forget it and how it made me feel. Jeremy began causing a scene in the store and attempted to fight the boy. As we drove back home, he yelled at me, called me names and was really demeaning toward me. I felt like I was all the things Jeremy called me. I was very hurt because we were so close, and I broke his trust. He began looking at me differently and didn't talk to me the rest of his visit. He just cut me off; I never want to go through that again.

I think the most difficult time for me was when Jesse was incarcerated. It was hard because my parents were trying to get him out and help him financially, and I knew it was because of me. At Jeremy's wedding rehearsal dinner, he was giving remarks and said that his best man was supposed to be his big brother and he started crying. In that moment, I felt how that one decision I made in rage impacted the whole family.

I did try to find things to help me cope and express myself. I love writing poems, songs, and stories. I also like to draw and I even try to convince myself that I can dance. But my peace is in drawing. And talking to my grandmother; that is the one thing in this world that helps me deal with so much. Talking to her has made be able to sleep better at night and, even when she does not agree with me, she is able to talk to me in a calming way. She never would tell me what to do, but she would let me know how my choices would affect my life. I love my Mimi so much.

My other best friend Mia, I met in the 10th grade. We clicked immediately. We enjoyed being around each other. Her parents are sweet and involved. We talked about so many things and it wasn't just about boys. I really decided we were close friends when I told her Chris Brown was going to be my husband and she was completely on board. We had great times together.

FROM A MOTHER TO A WARRIOR

From Jeremy…

The move to Georgia with my family happened during the summer when I was going to the 2nd grade and I was seven years old. The only memory I am able to recall was that one of my dad's older brothers helped us pack up, and one of his younger brothers came to help us move into our new house. I didn't even realize that we were moving until after we got to Georgia and brought in our things. My parents had told us at some point that we would be moving, but I didn't understand that this meant we would actually be separated from our other family. I think it was easy for me because my siblings and my parents were all together.

I know now as an adult that every family has their issues and everyone sees things differently, but what was difficult in our family was not having freedom to go to sleepovers, going on trips with friends, and not having a chance to stay out late. My mom was very strict when it came to those types of activities.

On the other hand, the good times were when we went on a trip to Universal Studios with my mom's best friend and her family. They would come from Indiana, stay with us a few days and we would all travel together. Even though they were not blood family, it was like my mom's friend was her sister and her kids were my cousins. We had not been on trips with anyone outside of family, which made those trips fun.

One of my favorite childhood memories is my mom not allowing us to have a dog. My dad was all for it, but she refused to allow us to have one. I remember my mom showing us a picture of some puppies and she told us she was taking us to pick one out. I just flipped! The day we picked him out and named him Buddy was the best day of my childhood.

The one time as a child when I really felt proud was me playing basketball for the recreation team. I was in about the 5th or 6th grade and my grandmother came to one of my basketball games. She had never been able to see me do something that I enjoyed outside of being around the family. I didn't have a relationship with any other grandparent and having her there made me feel good.

There was a time when our family had to move into apartments and we were not going to be able to take Buddy. My parents told us he was going to have to be put to sleep. I was very sad because we had watched him grow from a newborn. Another sad time in my life was when my brother got in trouble. I knew it was bad, but I didn't know how bad it was going to be. We were leaving school one day and Jesse came to the window at the bus and told me to get off the bus because there is going to be a fight, but the driver wouldn't let me off. My brother knew he was going to be in a fight and fighting was not something we did. That was the last memory I have of seeing him before he went to jail. I felt really bad that I couldn't be there for him like he needed. During this time, I started getting closer to my sister and pulling away from my parents.

FROM A MOTHER TO A WARRIOR

I had a close friend that I would talk to everyday. He was very positive and helped me through some really rough times. I also began dating my high school sweetheart, who is now my wife. I started attending their church and I wanted to go to events and church retreats, but my parents didn't let me participate. I felt they were jealous of the girlfriend. I liked being away from the house and experience things like eating Chinese food or going to the waterpark with friends. I felt like my girlfriend's family exposed me to other races and cultures.

My mom was really mean and strict, while my dad was the soft one. It seemed like I could only talk to my dad when my mom was at work. Now as an adult, I wish I had not rushed to be away from my parents and that I had stayed in school longer. I thought it was mean of them that they would not allow me to go to summer retreats. I knew I was in summer school almost every summer, but I wanted to be with my girlfriend and it seemed that my parents were trying to keep us separated.

During my teenage years, it seemed that my dad was very aggressive towards me. I didn't know if it was because of my brother's issues or if he was just angry about stuff. He was easily aggravated and he just wouldn't talk about what was bothering him. At Christmas and when it was time for school to start, my grandparents would send us money and my mom would take it from us. I felt like my mom was robbing us. She would take the money and tell us it would be used for when we needed but when we wanted the money, she would tell us there wasn't any money left. I never thought about how we were still able to get almost everything we wanted.

When my brother went to jail, I had to take on the role of the oldest sibling, but I was conflicted between that role and being a boyfriend. I must say that my parents did give me guidelines for making mistakes and picking my friends. There were times that I felt neglected as the middle child — they were always worried about Jesse because of his legal issues and worried about my sister because she was the youngest. They even took time to care about Hope's future by planning for her to go to a private school but with me, it was like I was just there.

After high school, I really felt like "what now?" My parents gave me a few options and none of them seemed to be appealing. One day I went to Publix to get an update on my application and they were not interested in me. I saw a military poster and went in to get information. I didn't feel like college was really for me, but I wanted a job that gave me meaning. The Navy told me I couldn't get the job I wanted, but the Army was able to get me in immediately.

I had six months before I had to leave for basic training. I was afraid of so many things like my relationship coming to an end; not seeing my parents; and I had never been on my own before where I didn't know anyone. I thought about being lonely. This was the scariest time of my life. While on the bus leaving that day, I was typing a letter on my cell phone to everyone. The letter was thanking my parents and telling them how much I love them and before I knew it, I went to sleep. When I woke up, life was real. All I heard was yelling and screaming. I had arrived at basic training.

When I graduated from basic training, I treasured everything ten times more. I knew I wanted to marry my girlfriend. Completing this process was a big accomplishment for me. I really felt I would be able to make it without my parents.

As an adult man, I believe my mom is proud of who I am. She has been there for me throughout high school, graduation, joining the Army and getting married. I now see a lot of things that my mom went through while we were young, like going to college while taking care of us and working multiple jobs. I remember she couldn't come to some of my football games because she had to work or do homework. I am able to see the results of those sacrifices, like her being a therapist and owning her own business. My mom is always full of advice and guidance and she always talks about our family legacy.

My mom gave me the very love languages I needed: touch and quality time. Both my mom and her mom did this the most which always made me feel loved by them. Love from my dad was through gifts. My dad knew all my favorite snacks and he knew everything I liked and how to get me. Dad would tell me how much he loved me all the time while we were riding in the car together. Although my dad was really rough, he would still let me know how proud he was of me.

I know Jesse loves me. Before he went to jail, we always spent time and did things together. Everyone knew me at school as "Jesse's little brother." He was very popular. When Jesse came home, our relationship was completely different; he wanted me with him all the time. Even now when I meet his friends they tell me that Jesse talks about me. My brother just wants to spend time with me.

Hope's love for me is easy and simple, she makes me feel needed. She talks to me about everything all the time. She is very possessive of me and wants all my time. I know my sister loves me.

In conclusion, I would tell the parents of a middle child to be patient and there is a reason why they are doing what they are doing. I would tell my younger self: that it is going to be alright. You will go through life trying to show people that you are here.

To my family,

I love each and every one in my family, and with all that we've been through we have still managed to overcome. I realize that the fight is not over but I know we can overcome anything.

To my Mimi, thank you for everything you've sent my way. Thank you for being there every step of my life, you are like a second mother to me. To my Pawpaw, I wish you could have been in my life more and I could have spent more time with you and got to know you more while I was young.

From Jesse...

I love my family and I'm thankful for how my mom and dad have supported me and been there for me. Growing up in this family was difficult because I was not allowed to go to parties and hang out with friends. School was always difficult for me, but I really loved being in band during high school and I didn't realize how much of a difference it made in my life when we moved and I was not able to participate any more. I loved playing the drums and meeting people who did the same thing I enjoyed. I always looked forward to football games and competitions. Working out is something I liked doing in high school as well; I became obsessed with it. Dressing for school when I was in high school was fun and made me feel good. Every night I would try on three or four outfits, press my clothes and be ready to go the next day.

The other issue that was hard was not being around family members like all my grandparents and great grandparents. I feel like I should have spent more time with them. The best time in the family for me was traveling on vacations when we went to Florida, different beaches and home to visit family. I loved Christmas time with the family and being in Indiana where we were able to see more family. I can remember my dad telling us that he got a job in Georgia and we would be moving. I remember thinking that we would be missing our family.

The best childhood memory I had was in middle school when the band teacher let me play in a drum battle against my friend. The saddest time for me was when I went to jail and could not see my family. I believed God was going to get me out of that situation and I stood on faith. My parents and grandparents helped me get out. I felt bad that my family had to spend so much money on me for that. Life was hard for me trying to get through school and get a job that paid enough money for me to pay my bills.

I missed going to my prom, but a friend asked me to go to hers and it was so much fun. I remember my mom taking a lot of pictures and it seemed like after that I couldn't stop taking pictures of myself. I found a love in modeling and taking pictures and have always wanted to be a personal trainer.

My brother and I were very close when we were younger, and I loved us being around each other all the time even though we fought about clothes and games. After I got out, it seemed like we became distant. I wish we could be tighter, but he is married and doesn't live close to us since he has been in the Army.

My sister is the baby of the family. She is spoiled and doesn't even know it. She is annoying and acts like a girl by talking a lot. I love her and I always try to do what I can to make her happy.

To my family...

I love my mom because she is a protector and is always thinking of ways to help me when I am struggling. She corrects me when I make mistakes. My mom is very strict but the one thing I have learned is from her is persistence. I watch my mom spend a lot of time with work and school and I want to be that way about my goals.

My dad stays on my case. I love to be around him, and I think he loves being around me but I always felt like I was forced to work with him in his business so I could take care of my business. I learned a lot from him about being a man and a father. My friends would always tell me how good I had it with the way my parents supported me.

My Pawpaw is so cool and funny. He makes me laugh and likes to give us advice. He remembers us every Christmas and birthday.

Mimi is the calm person in the family. She is quiet and seems to stay to herself. One thing about her is that she doesn't play around with people. Mimi always spends time with us and shows me that she cares about me. After we moved to Georgia, she came to pick us up every summer and break. She would take us school shopping and to the Expo. I remember watching her take care of her mom and telling her, "I want you to take care of me when I get old like that."

I want to tell other guys to listen to their parents and think twice before making a decision. I don't like talking about what I've been through but trust me, you don't want to experience it.

From My Husband…

FROM A MOTHER TO A WARRIOR

Unlike so many of my peers, I did not get married until I was 30 years old. I was never in a rush to get married. When I met the woman who God showed me was my wife, I was excited about taking on the next chapter of getting to know the woman who would be a part of me. The first ten years of our marriage was spent in our hometown. My wife and I never dated so we did not have time to get to know each other. We instantly became parents the first year of our marriage, which meant that we were learning each other while learning how to parent.

Our first several years were very challenging and felt much like a power struggle. I thought that I was ready and able to take care of my family. I had a mind to be a provider for my family although I didn't have anyone teaching me how because my dad was not there for me in that way. I didn't have uncles that were calling me or teaching me how to be a father or husband. Because I did not see this, I had to grow up and figure this part out for myself.

Growing up in a family of five brothers and a single mother made life very hard and did not teach me how to manage finances for myself or a family. After being married and being able to acquire material things in life, I finally felt free and I did not feel a need to get permission about my spending. This kept a lot of contention in our marriage. I felt that moving to Georgia would give us a fresh start and be a great opportunity financially. We moved from an apartment that was bigger than the house we had. Then we were able to buy our first brand new home. It was in a very nice community and the pool was right across the street. The home was a five bedroom in a new community. I had never been in this place in my life before and it made me feel like we had made major accomplishments.

I felt our marriage and family was in a good place. At this period in our life we didn't have any issues. We took trips to the coast frequently. We were introduced to a church by some friends and became very active. I went to church when I was growing up and it was very important to me to have my family in church as well. We were able to develop friends. I felt that God was using me, but I felt there was so much more that not only I needed to be doing in ministry but that the ministry needed to be doing. When we left that church to start our ministry, I felt relieved in so many ways because there would be opportunities to reach out to the community through a food pantry and assist homeless families. When we had to close our ministry, I felt hurt, oppressed, and distressed. I kept seeking God to find out why I was in this place. I felt God had turned his back on me and I didn't want to talk to my wife or anyone. I didn't even want to go to church. I was in a very dark place.

I wanted a lot of things that I was not able to have when I was much younger. My wife kept telling me that we needed to watch our spending. I started spending excessively, buying the kids whatever they wanted because I didn't have that luxury when I was growing up. Through my excessive spending, I stopped being consistent with paying the mortgage. This made life difficult for my children and wife and I could not even see it. At Christmas, we would plan on what we would get the children, but I was never satisfied with that. I would buy more gifts because I didn't get much at Christmas for myself as a child. Because of my excessive spending, we lost our beautiful home. In the midst of trying to keep the house, I was scammed. I abused the finances and I still reflect on the hurt that I caused on my family.

Living in Georgia took me away from my family. My mother did not come to Georgia which is the one thing that I missed the most. When we were having very hard times financially, I could not call on anyone in my family for help. My wife's mother was a life saver for us and my relationship with her was very important to me. I never felt that my wife's mother treated me in any bad way and she loved on me the same as she did her daughter. Through the years, our relationship has grown and I enjoy calling her just to talk, ask questions, get a recipe or discuss the NBA Playoffs. My father-in-law has also helped us throughout the years. I can honestly say that the last several years we have gotten closer and I love him coming to visit. The only problem I ever have with my father-in-law is when we cannot agree on the best NBA players.

My oldest son Jesse was special because he was born having to fight for his life. He is the child that taught us how to be parents. Jesse is one child that is kind-hearted and very forgiving. Despite of everything he has been through, he really is a good son. Jesse has spent the most time with me because he has worked with me in my landscaping business. Because of what Jesse has been through as a teenager and how he lost so much of his youth and young adult life, I felt that as a father, I needed to pour into him as much as I could so that if anything ever happened to me, he would be more aware of life. My biggest frustration with Jesse is his lack of applying what we teach him. Honestly, with Jesse I had to learn a lot of patience and I'm still learning, but there is no way I could ever give up on my own son.

My namesake, Jeremy, is also my baby boy. I see so much of myself in Jeremy. As a baby, he cried for me all the time and was attached to my hip. Jeremy was most challenging when he came into his teen years. He wanted so much independence and started detaching from us. He would come home past curfew, be disrespectful, and not want to be at home. He was very social and loved being active. Jeremy, unlike Jesse, was the child that tried us. I felt that he always wanted to challenge me physically. I was very happy for him and proud of him when he enlisted in the Army. I really couldn't wait to see changes in his life. When he told me that he had decided to get married, I felt upset because I really thought he was rushing. I was mad and pissed when he came home from the courthouse. I felt he and I was much closer than that and I could not believe that he went through with it without me. All-in-all, I couldn't be prouder of him because he was man enough to make his decision.

"Daddy's Ping-Pong Girl Y'all." My princess. As much as I love Hope, she tries my patience. She learned at an early age how to manipulate me and play me against my wife. When I thought I really knew her as she was going into her teen years, her behavior showed me that I didn't know her at all. I learned that girls think and do things very differently than boys. I love the fact that my daughter will come to me to talk about a variety of topics. She is not scared to ask me questions about boys, what to do, and even what she may have done wrong. I see so many gifts and talents in Daddy's girl. I don't think she sees her abilities and her worth the way that I do and as a father, I have always tried to encourage her.

In conclusion, I have learned so much from my family even though we have been through so much. God has taught me how to trust Him. I pray that this book will give people hope to listen to each other and lift up one another during trying times.

I would like to express to all fathers to communicate with your children, make time in your life for them and listen to them. Talk to your sons about life and how to be a husband and father. Do not put them in a position where they have to learn this on their own, I've been there and it is not a good place. Husbands, pay attention to what your wife is doing within the family. There was so much I could have done to lessen the load for my wife that I did not see until years later. Take the time to pour into your wife words of affirmation, appreciation and never take her for granted. Let her know that you are listening and that you see her. My wife has not only been a mother to our children, but she has turned into the warrior our family needed most during our time of turmoil.

Terri L. White

Warriors

In everything that I've been through, I praise God. It's just what I do. I love my family so much and I cannot imagine these three children having to have gone through life without their parents fighting and advocating for them. My children did not make the best decisions, and yes, some of their decisions cost our family some real tears, anxiety, frustration and great disappointment. So many times, I could hear God in the midst of those various challenges saying, "But you can take it, anchor down and show me what's in you. You are a warrior."

As we work to build this legacy of empowerment, restoration, faith and love for our children and their children, I pray that generations to come will be able to talk about the foundation we laid and what we had to do to lay it.

The one piece of knowledge that I can say for certain God gave me is this: my trials were never about me. They were never about my kids. It was all for the people who read this book to know they are not alone. Yes, you may go through some challenges within your family but that is exactly why God has placed so many people just like me in this world to help you and your family be restored.

Parents, if you are struggling with your children's behavior, their way of thinking, their attitude of disrespect, it is time for you to tap into the warrior within. Lean on your support system, get a counselor if you need one. It's okay to ask for help, no one can do it all alone.

Don't doubt what God has placed inside of you. Anchor down and don't give up. Do not give in to what you see, hear or feel. Look to the cross. "In all things God works for the good of those who love him, who have been called according to his purpose." Romans 8:28

We are victorious in Christ!

ABOUT THE AUTHOR

"Breaking the Silence" and "From a Mother to a Warrior" is the work of Terri L White, who is a Licensed Professional Counselor for the state of Georgia. Terri does not hold back when it comes to being transparent and helping Christian families and couples to move through difficult challenges. She is not only a Relationship Expert who enjoys speaking and training couples as well as those who work with couples, but a Certified Trainer through Prepare-Enrich and her own relationship curriculums, Breaking Generational Strongholds in Marriages, Almost Married and Relationships Under Fire.

Terri is a wife of over 25 years, a mother of three and soon to be a "Nana". While she is currently attending Capella for her Doctorates in Human Services, Specializing in Nonprofits, her Master's was obtained from Liberty University in Professional Counseling and Bachelors of Business from Northwood University.

This multi-talented author and speaker has launched her solo counseling practice White Diamond Counseling Consulting Coaching, LLC in 2015 which transitioned to a Family Systems Group practice in 2018, where she serves in the heart of downtown Lawrenceville, GA. Entrepreneurship is something Terri embraces which allowed her to create an online training business, Advanced Education and Training.

Terri L. White

FROM A MOTHER TO A WARRIOR

www.ingramcontent.com/pod-product-compliance
Lightning Source LLC
Chambersburg PA
CBHW071408290426
44108CB00014B/1736